Cumberland Station

Books by Dave Smith

Cumberland Station
The Fisherman's Whore
Mean Rufus Throw Down
Drunks (chapbook)
Bull Island (chapbook)

Cumberland Station

Poems by
DAVE SMITH

University of
Illinois Press

Urbana
Chicago
London

Grateful acknowledgment is made to the Board of Trustees of Western Michigan University for a grant in creative writing which enabled me to complete a portion of this collection.

Second printing, 1979

Manufactured in the United States of America

Library of Congress Cataloging in Publication Data

Smith, David Jeddie, 1942–
    Cumberland Station.

    I. Title.
PS3569.M5173C8   811'.5'4   76-13582
ISBN 0-252-00581-3
ISBN 0-252-00582-1 pbk.

Many of the poems collected here first appeared in the following publications, to whose editors grateful acknowledgment is made for permission to reprint:

Ascent: "The Delivery"

Carolina Quarterly: "Si Hugget, Drifting, Ruptured"

Chariton Review: "Undertaker, Please Go Slow"

Chicago Review: "Pink Slip at Tool & Dye" "Driving Home in the Breaking Season" "With Walt Whitman at Fredericksburg" "In the City of Wind" "The Sex of Poetry"

Greensboro Review: "The Cunner in the Calotype"

Hudson Review: "One Question, Two Seasons" "The Gift of the Second Snow"

Jam To-Day: "Eastern Shore: Smith Island" "The Last Morning"

Kansas Quarterly: "The Austringer's Dissertation"

Kayak: "The Divorce"

Midwest Quarterly: "The Ancestor" "The Testimony of Wine"

Minnesota Review: "A Poem While It Is Raining"

The Nation: "Lee's Statue: Richmond"

New Yorker: "Cumberland Station" "On a Field Trip at Fredericksburg" "Sailing the Back River" "The Perspective and Limits of Snapshots" "The Funeral Singer" "Looming: An Address to Matthew Fontaine Maury" "Looking for the Melungeon" (originally "Shack Song")

North American Review: "When the Fiddlers Gather"

Northwest Review: "Hole, Where Once in Passion We Swam"

Ohio Review: "Small Song for Breadloaf " (originally "The Levitator")

Perspective: "The Palmreader"

Prairie Schooner: "Something the Wind Says Tonight"

Poetry: "Dome Poem"

Poetry Northwest: "Blues for Benny Kid Paret"

Puddingstone: "Coming Attractions" "How to Get to Green Springs"

Shenandoah: "Night Fishing for Blues" "The Luminosity of Life" "Figure from an Elder Lady" "Some Good Luck in Lightfoot"

Southern Poetry Review: "Snake Sermon" "Picking Cherries"

Sou'wester: "Drunks" "Pietas: The Petrified Wood" "For the Polioed Girl Killed by Cottonmouths on Her Birthday"

Windsor Review: "First Hunt at Smithfield"

To My Family, This Book

Above children, over the herd
of plastic animals, the armaments,
our angel keeps its shy place.
Something of its silence works
to ease our daily discontents.
Mostly, though, it waits.
We hardly look at it.

We call it *thing*. It hovers,
tucked tight as the lightning
bug in our fists, stilled
as we are in sometime fevers.
I touch it now for one who sings,
the woman who scoffs at angels,
yet nailed up the thing.

Contents

The Seamen call it *looming*. Philosophy is as yet in the rear of the seamen, for so far from having accounted for it, she has not given it a name. Its principal effect is to make distant objects appear larger, in opposition to the general law of vision, by which they are diminished. I knew an instance at Yorktown, from whence the water prospect eastwardly is without termination, wherein a canoe with three men, at a great distance was taken for a ship with its three masts.

Thomas Jefferson
Notes On The State Of Virginia

Part I

The Last Morning

Alone in the camp, all others dumb
with the humming sleep of the reeds
and the dew so thick in their hair
it flashes like brilliant insects,
I get up and go down to the river.

The current skeins the bottom stones
with pale, early light, the cold flow
that cries to the sea-borne salmon
come, my friend, come and be still.
In the earth, tree roots are listening.

Taking two stones I pound my shirt
like a woman whose knees are slick
after long kneeling; the arms float
away from me and the chest swells.
It is that easy to begin a passage.

Later I sit naked, clothing the trees
with shirt and pants that want wind.
It is then across water a wolverine
comes to drink and a trout dimples
the silence like the soul rising. I

begin to hear not far away the crash
of dammed water and a beaver's bark.
I think unaccountably of an early snow,
children with black, hungry eyes, men
cutting arrows where the elders bud.

Pietas: The Petrified Wood

An old cottonwood has jeweled, my piece
the bruise of a warrior's first spear
hurtled, retrieved as the sun circles
and a boy hardens to a man.
I touch it to see him learn the art
of killing, and a man grows
to a boy in the presence of scars.

It does not live, on my desk,
in its warm grains, would not burn,
though it is filled with smoke,
or slowly bear the agonizing green
of a desert spring. But as heartwood
I keep it for its weight, its shape
showing where the lance entered
and currents of sap loosed, shone,
broke the winter bark each year

as a man and a boy run down an arroyo
illusory with heat, tufts of dust
growing under their feet, the haze
of spring spreading like a sweat.
My finger sees the spear cocked
up like a bird toward the horizon
and I know the angle is still wrong
where a man grins up at the light
leaves, his arms open as if to soar,
and I feel the gouged bark fall, and
fall again, already beginning to be
mine, a spice in the dry air.

First Hunt at Smithfield

Pulling in we're careful to be quiet, don't shut
doors, ease everything, careful as we cock
the Winchesters. No good, the farmer's bitch licks
a chain of barks, dirty chickens sound the alert.
                          You smoke. He's
up anyway because it's never early for a man
whose skin wakes without the lie of clocks.

A black snake slithers off the road we take,
his muscles ticking dew.
                    To me, to you, is it the same
high weaving green, boil of yellows, black trunks of oak?
Where our road ends you angle off, camouflaged
almost, and almost hang like an aging leaf
under the eddying light, a shadow on that slope.
I hardly hear you whisper *here* but feel
my buttocks take the rotting trunk. What words
I had to bite back, thousands it seemed.

You sweep the air like a hawk and load.

I know you'll calculate my shots, my time, unbreak
your father's double, portion out the shells. Will I
do it right? So many things to think about,
each one my need to please you.
                          I watched the gray
creep in a fickle drift at your temple. I made
my eyes track the trees like yours. I learned
each knob, each distant sound, the way morning heat
tricked the wet leaves to sing with snapping, how

one shape implies a family, a line in wait.

                    The guns bent my bones
when you were done. It was a long road back.
You dumped their bodies in a pile. Cold water

washed the tufts of fur from my small knife. Later
you tendered the farmer meat and smoked awhile
on the step of his truck. What you said was gone
before I heard it. I watched for that deep act
to pass between us, not knowing what it was. Dreaming

the dingy sinews of all those guts, the nights
played the same tune until I knew you well. I always
scrubbed the guns when we got home, made coffee
below the stairs, until your chair
stopped rocking, and your snore.

—for Harry M. Cornwell

The Ancestor

How well I know him, old soldier in blue
Union suit that might have been fireman's show
duds on the day they burned the whorehouse down.
Captain of the hosing team, he sprayed crowds,
the settees, the porch, but let others scorch
handlebars and muttonchops. Not his torch.
He'd be damned, maybe, but he'd sin enough,
death, fire, and fear, too, at Antietam's bluffs.
Under him, I lie in grandfather's house,
bird-fat for holidays, deepsick of grouse,
television news, lies, repeated rapes
by puffing gents without girls, knowing ropes
bounce the way they always did, but more, worse.
Framed over faces that mumble this day's curse,
his face, distant as a moon, scarred, boot-scuffed,
but oddly close, a face that still spits, gruffs,
sits straight, that brittle god with bad back pain,
gutshot by the past, present, future, flames
brazing each brass button. Our whores have names.
Brothers, fathers look up for his signals
but cold Buck's locked hard dumb in his Eagles.

—for Asham Buckner

7

With Walt Whitman at Fredericksburg

after Louis Simpson

I have brought the twittering flags old bear-hug,
the swaying noose you admired at the end
of the 13th Brooklyn muskets sashaying
down Broadway, everybody's intended girl
swooning, Jesus, for the grandeur of it.

I have brought a tumbler of spring water
for the sipping if your brother George lives.

I see you and Simpson stepping carefully through
wreckage, the hacked-off arms, useless with Masonic
rings, for God's sake, shining like used-car lots.
The arms are so American, like parts junked
before the expiration of their longevity.
This is no joke for Velsor Brush to peddle.

I have brought a red handkerchief
for our mouths. Godalmighty, the stink grows.

I've come here like you to pick a way to the heart
of the business, tracing out what ripples I can,
skirting blood pooled like knocked-over
coffee on my own sunny backporch. But
I see you and Simpson arm wrestling
in a lantern's moon, sighing out
the lonely words of America's losses.

I wish I could say it was December 13, 1862,
but the faces of young men I see aren't Christ,
dead and divine, and brother of all, though
they wear the green clothes of Park Rangers,
the polite smile of Toledo, and one
thinks you sold him a Buick.

Isn't it for them we threw the noose in a can?
I gave George's water to a small boy found

8

by his mother in time, the life saved
he thought lost, which he will lose again.

If you lay your body down in this Virginia green,
you feel the quick shadows of tourists, the whispers
that zing in your stomach like miniballs or
knee-high bees. Loafing like this
you can hear the freeway moaning under ground
dry and beige as free-shrunken coffee,
or look up into the drained, tossing leaves
of October. Alone on a stolen Army blanket

I've stretched out a long time here
to dig from a bright afternoon the glazed eyes
of anyone whose temple, as I touch it to clean
away the smear of ice, breaks my heart.

At dusk I may be the only one left to drift
down Marye's Heights where the Rappahannock mist rolls
over rocks humped like bodies, little dunes
inside which a black tide I cannot see
goes on rising and falling. I want

to tell you how progress has not changed us much.
You can see breaking on the woods the lights
of cars and the broken limbs glow
in the boomed rush of traffic that chants
wrong, wrong, wrong, wrong.

On a Field Trip at Fredericksburg

The big steel tourist shield says maybe
fifteen thousand got it here. No word
of either Whitman or one uncle
I barely remember in the smoke
that filled his tiny mountain house.

If each finger were a thousand of them
I could clap my hands and be dead
up to my wrists. It was quick
though not so fast as we can do it
now, one bomb, atomic or worse,
one silly pod slung on wing-tip,
high up, an egg cradled
by some rapacious mockingbird.

Hiroshima canned nine times their number
in a flash. Few had the time
to moan or feel the feeling
ooze back in the groin.

In a ditch I stand
above Marye's Heights, the book-
boned faces of Brady's fifteen-year-old
drummers, before battle, rigid
as August's dandelions
all the way to the Potomac
rolling in my skull.

If Audubon came here, the names
of birds would gush, the marvel
single feathers make
evoke a cloud, a nation,
a gray blur preserved
on a blue horizon, but

there is only a wandering child,
one dark stalk snapped off
in her hand, held out to me.
Taking it, I try to help her
hold its obscure syllables
one instant in her mouth,
like a drift of wind
at the forehead, the front door,
the black, numb fingernails.

Lee's Statue: Richmond

Ponderous, hanging in that bricked
circle, lord of cobblestones,
where the city's grit flecks,

the horseman seems to be running
a country's life, sword naked,
horse heroic, kicking free.

But someone has stuck like a bib
a note under his brass breast.
Or is it only the eviction

paper of a woman who cannot swallow
magnolias and eat muffins
any longer? Yellowed,

crisp as the early letters
which were months reaching those
at home with the good news

of freedom, it offends
in the craw of the Monument
Street crowd. They will extend

new efforts with sighs unmuffled.
That is one way to see it.
Another way is that of shuffling

collar up to the James River,
to blazing barrels and lies
older than Camptown races. There

the poster eye of a dark trotter
nailed to a gray-splintered wall
winks over a bottle.

Snake Sermon

In this picture you will see
Big Stone Gap, Virginia, the white
petals of dogwood blurred back
of the woman standing in what
we call the nave. She lifts
the snake, a moccasin, mouth pure
as cream when it opens, the shade
of Daddy's inner thigh. It ought
to be a rattler, big diamonds
chaining her throat like beads,
a tail to shake hell out of those
windows that overlook nothing.
But it's only black, thick
as horse cock in her little fingers,
its tongue licking the silence
out of the rough pews. You can't
buy rattlers anymore, big dozers
drove them away to prairies and
the snatching hands of farm boys
in sweat-belted baseball hats.
Times change, even way in here.
One cottonmouth per Sunday now,
bless the Lord for his bounty.
Three for Easter and Christmas.

For the Polioed Girl Killed by Cottonmouths
on Her Birthday

d. May, 1960, Virginia Beach, Virginia

On her birthday in the green-glowing May of each year
I hobble in my head to that ocean-side carnival
where she is screaming near the thrash
of winter's last indifferent surf,

close my eyes and one stunningly
soft face in my brain's room stands up,
comes alive with the fuse of birthday candles,
glows incandescent with a beauty nothing can snuff out.

I stand ghostly behind parents I can never see, unseen,
they who placed their three-years living child
in the heart of a split-hoofed, musically
metal stallion, strapped her down

that she might never fly wildly
with her own loosed heart. Again the nod
to one who controls a lever, who sets teeth in
motions like the great gears of almighty God. Again I

must see her eyes widen with the slow planet-like sail
of that iron paddock plate, again,
convulsively hooked deep in her breath,
feel skull powder and powerful hurt flood her

veins like the backsurge of oceans tumbling down and
through the nerves of suddenly terrified
swimmers. Clenching her child, I
still hear the woman whisper *It's only fear, only fear.*

Around and around she rides posing for a bulb's flash,
no leverage in this world enough to help her
unsay what she had not yet learned to
fear, their words: *She'll live*

all summer on this, on her body's
joy flying, will take on delight's blood
buoyant shape of fish, duck and vaulting horse.
They said let her go, after church that soft Sunday,

on the first day of her fourth year. Even in her prayers
what could be better for a girl than a canter?
Oh the fear that whirled in that heart!
Each year I feel despair bite

with its life-saving needle-
teeth up and down her useless legs,
legs shackled to stand if only someone will
hold her two tiny arms up, feel her flesh try to say

how it needs help to stand suddenly on rubber bones
that cannot run from the thousand snakes
that all winter no one has prayed
into church. Useless despair,

for we know father-shriek but not
how to reach out in May for a mild girl
caught, trapped in surf-thunder and the easy
wheel of love whose horse circles blindly by the sea.

Not mother or father or lover of the woman she was not
ever to be, I do not know even her name or
why a nest of snakes came to live
near a child's tiny stable. If

I call it an accident of Spring,
a sad, blind misunderstanding of cold-blooded
beings hungry for the joy of their young, a woman-
child still doomed, refuses to throw off bindings, to get

up by the sea with sea wind in her hair and flee poison
meaner than the teeth-sucking joy-boys who

caretake the levers and gears of God's
dumb designs. What then? Something

so hideous of intent it must fester
in mud-stink and be unknown to a self-steeled
father striking shot after shot to hold onto his love
for his first girl come to ride out the day of her birth?

Tonight, not even the anniversary of that time when she
sagged for joy, fear-pierced, spun loose from
her life, another child screams, dying
maybe for snakebite or bad legs

or Daddy. As stranger I throb
with that hurt tonight, every night, and
I lift my fist in the air like Spring's rebellion
in May for children no man, no god loves enough to save.

The Austringer's Dissertation

You cannot get him easily, or you can so
easily what you get will be hardly
anything you'd want.

What you would wheedle for, of course, is
one with blood, a pulse in the throat,
claws which could cuddle eggs

or slice off the nails of your yellow toes.
To coax a thing like that from an air
rampant with colors like a cloak

worn, maybe, by a pedagogue or a Pope
requires that you have sifted your stock
item by item and have found

no stance but respect for his escapability.
Oh, you could take a scatter-gun approach
for a lot of meat and feathers

or adopt a bigger bird and cross your fingers.
There are many who advocate both,
and some that sigh "Oh hell"

as they gayly trot out their personal butchers:
poisoned heartmeat, traps like existence
with cul-de-sacs and tiny bells

to wake them up should anything be caught.
Many merely hunt, never knowing where.
If you like soft hours this

crowd's for you. The best sift dung and may
work years alone without a clue.
Then: the shadow, a fine

phrase in high fir, slight beating of a heart,
shift of a seed on a summer's day,
and all doubt

17

dissolves, as a taste of gun steel in your mouth
leaves Truth. That is when work begins,
the real, winds, hours, the lies

you crack like pretzels for an emperor of air.
What it will get you mostly is dead
and few who'll pull your boots.

How to Get to Green Springs

Nobody knows exactly when it fell off the map
or what the pressures were on its flooding river.
The hedge, the tottering mailbox were gone. That dimple
of light from the bicycle that raised itself to creak
at noon across a clattering bridge names my father.
His blood silent as a surging wish drags this town
lost through my body, a place I can get back to only
by hunch and a train whistle that was right on time.

But time and trains were never right in Green Springs,
West Virginia. What color could map the coal's grime,
shacks shored against the river every March, mail
left to rot because no one answered to occupant?
Farmers low on sugar cursed heat and left bad cigars
boys would puff back to clouds where they dreamed
of girls naked as their hands under outfield flies.
Scores were low. There were no springs for the sick.
Women lined their walls with the Sears catalog, but
the only fur they ever had was a warbled rabbit.
To get here think of dirt, think of night leaking,
the tick of waterbugs, a train held in Pittsburgh.

The Luminosity of Life

after Doris Ullman

All the mothers and fathers here in sickness,
in health, in Ullman's black-and-whites
pretend not to be dying. *Where are they?*

Look close at the head against the hickory,
that man who lies at the picnic's end
by his wife on their best bedsheet,
their eyes feigning sleep, closed.

When did that happen? Who are they?
They are about to wake up and father you.

What about the river they crossed? The same,
hardening somewhere, become a new road.

A certain light evokes itself, some distress
they never escape—you can't deny this.
Yes, it plays like the distant chords of banjos
tickling in a sleeper's dream

                    and, as Ullman saw,
endless, begun. Light on those child-mothers,
the roccoco coils of the weather-withered
boardinghouse in Tuscaloosa.
                    But who
speaks for that man about to crumple
backward when the chair legs break, the sun topples?
The fat woman, naked in the top corner window.

The silk in her lap, lustrous somehow (*Please?*),
somehow knows, doesn't give a damn for tomorrow,
which pretends it isn't ever coming back.

Every face in this land knows what a lie is.

Undertaker, Please Go Slow

Your fat wife weeps through her yellow shawl.
By bricks furred with soot your ragged cat laps
from a bottle then darts down the alley as if kicked.
The foreman cradles a clipboard with your name,
counting numbers from doors stained, God knows,
beyond any human use. The forklift yammers,

see, as I relive this moment of a morning
like a room full of machines suddenly stopped.
Today is Friday is what we learn fifty times
each year in the safety lecture and your name heads
the list of who gets reamed. You giggle *Zero*

defects is a prayer. The foreman's insults
tell us ice means a man needs more than good treads,
for Christ's sake, and blind fools cling to beds
of whores. Get some sleep, protect your eyes
with company lenses. We're engineered.

What happened to you? I don't know who I'm telling
how in last night's movie the words betrayed
the lips so I thought of lathes knocked out
of their smooth pigeon language. I want
a beer behind the door marked *No Trespassing.*

I mean to take every little bit of the good
advice any friendly yoyo wants to share
was what you said, and your dark wife weeps
while the liquored cat licks its dirty wounds.

When I rose up this morning I passed one man
I never saw who said it was a damn shame and I said
it was and no crap. Right there in the pouring
grit from Bethlehem's boiling stacks
that ate my own eyes, I said that

21

and said it again in the hanging city stink
while the sky came down like sheared tin over every
alky waking flopped and sick on the Pittsburgh asphalt,
and my boots said it all the way to the yard
where the forklift yammers in its teeth.

Blues for Benny Kid Paret

For years I've watched the corners for signs.
A hook, a jab, a feint, the peekaboo prayer of forearms,
anything for the opening, the rematch I go on dreaming.
What moves can say your life is saved?

> As I backpedaled in a field the wasp's nest waited,
> playing another game: a child is peeping out of
> my eyes now, confused by the madness of stinging,
> wave after wave rising as I tell my fists punish me,
> counter the pain. I take my own beating and God help

> me it hurts. Everything hurts, every punch
> jolts, rips my ears, my cheeks, my temples. Who hurts
> a man faster than himself? There was a wall to bounce
> on, better than ropes. I was eleven years old.

Eleven years ago I saw the fog
turn away and rise from the welts you were
to run away with its cousin the moon. They smacked
your chest and crossed your arms because you fell down
while the aisles filled with gorgeous women, high heels
pounding like Emille, the Champion, who planted his
good two feet and stuck, stuck, stuck, stuck
until your brain tied up your tongue and sighed.

> Somebody please, please I cried
> make them go away, but the ball in my hand had turned
> feverish with its crackling light. I could not let go
> as I broke against the wall. I was eleven years old.

Benny Paret, this night in a car ferrying
my load of darkness like a ring no one escapes,
I am bobbing and weaving in fog split only by a radio
whose harsh gargle is eleven years old, a voice in the air

telling the night you are down, counting time,
and I hear other voices from corners with bad moves say

Get up, you son of a bitch, get up! But you will not
get up again in my life where the only sign you give me

is a moon I remember sailing down on your heart
and blood growing wings to fly up in your eyes.
And there, there the punches no one feels grow weak,
as the wall looms, break through the best prayer you had
to dump you dizzied and dreaming in the green grass.

Cumberland Station

Gray brick, ash, hand-bent railings, steps so big
it takes hours to mount them, polished oak
pews holding the slim hafts of sun, and one
splash of the *Pittsburgh Post-Gazette*. The man
who left Cumberland gone, come back, no job
anywhere. I come here alone, shaken
the way I came years ago to ride down
mountains in Big Daddy's cab. He was
the first set cold in the black meadow.

Six rows of track gleam, thinned, rippling
like water on walls where famous engines steam, half
submerged in frothing crowds with something
to celebrate and plenty to eat. One engineer takes
children for a free ride, a frolic
like an earthquake. Ash cakes their hair.
I am one of those who walked uphill
through flowers of soot to zing
scared to death into the world.

Now whole families afoot cruise South Cumberland
for something to do, no jobs, no money for bars,
the old stories cracked like wallets.

This time there's no fun in coming back. The second
death. My roundhouse uncle coughed his youth
into a gutter. His son, the third, slid on the ice,
losing his need to drink himself
stupidly dead. In this vaulted hall
I think of all the dirt poured down
from shovels and trains and empty pockets.
I stare into the huge malignant headlamps
circling the gray walls and catch a stuttered
glimpse of faces stunned like deer on a track,
children getting drunk, shiny as Depression apples.

Churning through the inner space of this godforsaken
wayside, I feel the ground try to upchuck and I dig
my fingers in my temples to bury a child
diced on a cowcatcher, a woman smelling
alkaline from washing out the soot.
Where I stood in that hopeless, hateful room
will not leave me. The scarf of smoke I saw
over a man's shoulder runs through me
like the sored Potomac River.

Grandfather, you ask why I don't visit you
now you have escaped the ticket-seller's cage
to fumble hooks and clean the Shakespeare reels.
What could we catch? I've been sitting in the pews
thinking about us a long time, long enough to see
a man can't live in jobless, friendless Cumberland
anymore. The soot owns even the fish.

I keep promising I'll come back, we'll get out,
you and me, like brothers, and I mean it.
A while ago a man with the look of a demented cousin
shuffled across this skittery floor and snatched up
the *Post-Gazette* and stuffed it in his coat
and nobody gave a damn because nobody cares
who comes or goes here or even who steals
what nobody wants: old news, photographs
of dead diesels behind chipped glass
swimming into Cumberland Station.

I'm the man who stole it and I wish you were here
to beat the hell out of me for it because
what you said a long time ago welts my face
and won't go away. I admit
it isn't mine even if it's nobody else's.
Anyway, that's all I catch this trip—bad

news. I can't catch my nephew's life, my uncle's,
Big Daddy's, yours, or the ash-haired kids'
who fell down to sleep here after the war.

Outside new families pick their way along tracks
you and I have walked home on many nights.
Every face on the walls goes on smiling,
and, Grandfather, I wish I had the guts
to tell you this is a place I hope
I never have to go through again.

Driving Home in the Breaking Season

There is no need of maps now, the interstate spooling
south of Roethke's country
gone sour: smokestacks thick as the risen fists of
robber barons, the burly smudge
of green he sang choked out by the Tonka Toy houses
the same mile after mile. Even snow
surprising in April can't soften Flint, the gray pall
Buick slides over Ann Arbor. Creeks
like steel rods in the buff ground make me think of fish
stiff in the neck to Toledo. Wind-
drift and grit surging through Ohio, toward Pittsburgh.
Night, the bored disc jockey,
cackling bad jokes to keep us awake: sequence of motions
through toll booths, more
bad jokes counting the miles of rain into Pennsylvania
spring. Changing stations, I
discover I've gone wrong above Altoona. It's too cold to be
where I should be at this hour.
At the truck stop the sleepy kid doesn't understand why
he's 100 miles wrong and I spin
the dial for any music, turning south once more until
Maryland welcomes me and the lustery
shield of Rt. 40 says Cumberland sleeps 37 miles west, its
cupped coal hills hugging
the family bones we walked away from for the sea. Is it
high black air that makes me shiver
or a room with an all-night light and a plant unwatered?
Above D.C. a truckstop, eggs, coffee,
one fat waitress greasy at the end of her shift, winking
to teamsters pale as a slug's belly. They
still hate long hair. For one dumb, instinctive instant
I touch the book in my hip pocket,
then sag and pay up. If only one would listen, I could
make Roethke ring and coo

all the hurts they haul in their grinding loneliness. I
still think I could do that
at 2 A.M. when the high beams flick up to discover the red
cardinal of Virginia. I can't
shake snow from my head and take the off-ramp five miles
from Fredericksburg. Between trucks, two
hours of sleep. Cramped as if tucked in a father's body,
I dream a room of starch
and ammonia, a woman clucking me off to bed, a man hating
for the last time the coal dust. Then
for no reason on earth light batters in from all sides,
fog like brainfire, stillness
awakes. And, as if I knew it would be, there on a grass
slope dogwood blooming. Reason
enough to shake deep when a truck backfires beyond trees
like a howitzer. The whole luscious
green world welcomes us. Why go on hurting ourselves with
ash sealing the rivers of Saginaw?
Why serve the executives of Buick who hate trout? Think
of the gray birds at Fredericksburg
gorging on our mothers' sons and Roethke in his green war
gone like Whitman, bulldozed
like the secret river of the soul, but not ended, only
diverted, carving new banks. Poetry,
who watches you easing out along a timber stand, as I do,
dreaming the feel of trunk bark,
cradling the insults we make to God? To wake up glad
by a field alive with more than words,
the dead singing our wars remembered and unremembered, is
to love your life and give it
a way to rejoice. Isn't home the same everywhere, the open
room of the sea, your hands
slippery with all the fish the fathers haul in their nets?
Damn death. Today I do not believe
a single sparrow will die but I will croak back his life.

Part II

The Funeral Singer

Somewhere on a sideporch, in a viny haze of light,
you and I sift through pieces of a giant puzzle
to put together for once what must be
the Atlantic, a harbor unlikely
in the purest blue, a boat with a missing piece.

From a box of dark hand-rubbed hickory
music spools over our scratchy silence, the needle

sticks and when you flop back on the cool floor
I am gone into my white linen robe with stitches
of gold my mother made, constantly crossing herself.

The angelus cants in my mouth sometimes
like a tasteless wafer. Often I sing dreaming
what new puzzle my cash will buy

and later, missing notes because my voice cracks
over the open box I would never look into,
I break up in front of the puzzled faces of shifty
guards from St. Ignatius High, the same
bastards that took the all-city title
after spitting on our cheerleaders.

I take my cue from the other actor, his silence
after long speech I don't think anyone
truly hears. What did he mean
Render unto Caesar and the rest? I who am

the angel of song stand again in my wailing suit,
threadbare from years at the office,
cigarette burns, perhaps a little semen stain,

to make what one gaudy-cheeked woman said
was the road so many people needed
to find their way. In her foul breath
she hummed at my arm, croaking her thanks.

I didn't know any of those poor sons of bitches
who made me walk home thinking of a road out of town,
and I remember how once I broke down
sobbing harder than the great pipes.
They paid me double to hear me double their pain.

I only thought a girl was pregnant, whom I'd touched
wrongly and would die for, as the crow-footed nuns
flapped in their habits.

My voice was never half so good or pure as yours.
Probably you could, if asked, disinter each face,
recount how many points scored, where we lost
the piece with the head of the fisherman.

I've spent my whole life thinking we got screwed
by a maker of defective toys, learning
how not to hear my heart's
lonely knocked-up wheezing.

My God, how long does a man have to sing
to hear it be right just once, to ease out
some hope for the freckled kid whose
best give-and-go didn't make a diddly damn
though it beat me back to tears
long ago defeated as I croon at his wake?

Brother of the girl who needed no help from us
to conceive her own pains, my friend
today I sang maybe my last music
and bought a puzzle
of the entire charted world.

I promise even if I live to die
to get our colors in their right places, I won't
leave you alone under the vines until it's done,
until I sing like the most acute needle on earth
every note we dug out of those pressed grooves.

After Drinking Near Muskegon, Michigan

Sometimes I lie back down
in the morning
after I have splashed my face,
after eggs and cinnamon toast.
It is laziness, I know,
the act of a fool
who should do his work.
But I do it just the same.
In the cold I go to bed,
taking off only my boots,
and lay down my body
while the snow comes.
Sometimes like that
I do not believe the poems
I have written or read.
I hardly hear
anyone's language.
I lie with my chin
tight against my knees
and think of white fields,
how they stretch so easily
where I will never go.
I think also of the frosted
bones of a child resting
like me in a lazy drift,
waiting for someone to come,
to bend down and blow breath
like a happy, forgiving fog.
Sometimes I lie like that
all morning and whisper to
snow scratching the walls.

Small Song for Breadloaf

The girl was chosen at random. He pointed
for the mystical brunette behind her. As
in all crowds the distortions of distance
made her think he wanted her. So he did.
She was a ballerina, her toes were trained
to love grace and to spurn the simple boards
that in other guises were as high as any
worm might dream of rising. Her stability
had taught her to forget ideas, her heart
kept her floating like a fish's air sac.
She pumped and dreamed and pumped and held
for the long glide into sunset, just offstage.
But that afternoon coming down in midair
she felt she was near the nadir at last.
I think I'll go to a show she said to her
blonde hair. She wanted to feel life swirl
around the way a dying diabetic sneaks out
for cherry pie. The levitator comes in now
with his noisy, chattering finger. She rises
to the stage, to his hand, backstrokes in
the weeping willow fronds of her hair, sleeps.
We cannot see why or how it is done; deftly
his sword nicks her free, passes under breast,
buttock, thigh, and severs the dark cloud
between her gilded ankles and his slippers.
Then ideas fly back into her from every source,
ears, nose, mouth, and all the sly orifices,
until she gains back her weight and her sex.
The curtain closes and we all begin to cheer.
He will give her many children and great pain.

A Poem While It Is Raining

You climb in my arms and say
get me. I do,
I get you
with my face, my finger,
which wherever you are
turns to a rippling
laugh. On such days
I am more glad
than the mockingbird
with its mad mimic
for the rain that drives
you into my arms
like a broken wing.
I lift you up,
carry you from room to room.
I say somebody please
tell me what to do
with this gift.
I even pretend not to hear
you say how light
your body is in my grip.
I keep only the unspooling
laugh that sings
get me, and I do
with my nose, my mouth,
my one terrible finger
drawn across your heart
where breath goes on
like a gusting wind
and the rain is still
a room I can keep locked.

The Testimony of Wine

One day as the green grass sighed to the crow
I stepped onto shore's shoulder and left the sea
forever, and that is why sailors love me so.

Lanky and odd you may say I was, with hips slender,
a foreign accent, a gown like an antique dew.
I loved to dance. I had good teeth like a beaver.

How the girls groused and did go on is no secret.
I made their good men raise up from spring's tools,
with one glance I drew them to stuttered speech,

for there is no beauty such as mine. They poured
from rank hod and splintered hoe and hovel-tent.
My Lord, you are right to say I was devotedly wooed.

Night and day, by the scores I succored them.
I readily embraced their gods (which I do repent).
With a few of the weakest I may have lost my head

as in our gamboling we played the water's table.
But that, of course, was years ago. I was so new.
Shall I tell you how it was? Your poets fumbled

my fame so I hardly knew myself. A girl's head turns.
What wench they wished they chose and I became her.
I was the sheet spread for blessing a bride's bones,

or else I was the sun, too blinding to gaze upon.
Some sighed I was a cave. Some said I was the cry
of distress with tangled hair and legs unshaven.

I became the hacksaw blade, then the shackle's loop,
and when they came for me I was dark and shy and raw.
My circumstance was crude. What a girl must do,

she does, you understand. My seed thins, I droop.
Oh I do not dance, I do not dance! I want a man,
the slap by firelight, that gusty two-fisted brute

crossing himself with claws. In hotels I sit and hum,
I have my moments. But the heroes I loved are gone.
Kiss and pity me now, I am the metaphor of bums.

The Divorce

One of them had a dental appointment, an abscess
having suddenly appeared, and when they kissed it was
the last kiss. Their mouths tasted of dead trout.
Daddy said, "Mommy, the dentist is a kindly sport
who likes to breathe death and rumor in his drill.
Why don't you go this very afternoon?" The dentist
had often told Mommy and Daddy how poison in the teeth
is a good surprise. Undetected, it attacks the body
like a horde of ravenous ants, he said. But the heart
is wise and bolts tight when it hears the ant-oars
splashing up the canals, he added. Naturally, he said,
this is a fine thing for business and it pleased him
to be able to do battle in such a wonderful cause.
Mommy said she wasn't sure what life was all about
but if he could remove the putrid trout, she'd come.
Daddy smiled and sent her off to the bus. The dentist
cocked her back in his dreamy chair, strapped her in,
and began to fill her with gas. But the poison stuck,
Mommy told Daddy, so she would require more time.
As the days passed she would sit under the dentist's
gaze and dream of her portable television, the menu
she must prepare for the Elks' annual dinner, and
she would sing little songs to remind her to pay
the insurance premiums. As each session ended,
the dentist would climb off her, remove and clean
his drill, and have the nurse suggest again the need
to brush thoroughly and constantly. Leave nothing Mommy,
nurse kept saying, and for God's sake think of yourself.
So Daddy came home from work, did the dishes, waited
for Mommy to get rid of her ants, and began to wonder
what life was all about. One day, summoning courage,
he asked Mommy how her teeth were. Mommy broke her
dinner plate on her forehead and said that's the last
time I eat dead trout. You go get your own dentist.

The Delivery

This is a poem about Nature. No use trying
to hide it. A woman in a bright blue Datsun
eased to a stop under a weeping willow tree
along state road five near Albany, Ohio. She
stood for a time near a brook brown with oil,
her hands folded across her swollen belly,
listening, as it seemed, to the elders' moans
at the edge of a field some distance south.
She conceived it to be a sigh of pleasure,
she was not dumb; somebody had got fucked.
But there was little time for such remorse.
Their church was not hers. She lay down,
the oil feeling like silk under her legs,
from which she had removed all clothing.
In a trice she delivered herself, the thing
slipping into her alabaster hands so quick
she did not look, but tried to nurse. Nothing.
This was the golden slipper no one could
wear, its back broken, smelling of long walks.
After a while she threw it into the briars.
In the rear-view mirror of the blue Datsun
she saw her ugly stepsisters waltz, shining
like angels in the aisles of jumbo jets. Out-
side of Albany she remembered that somewhere
the Toad was waiting to be kissed. Shifting,
she sang. She did not feel the thumps burst
beneath the baby blue machine that hummed,
hovered through the melon fields and summer.

Something the Wind Says Tonight

Let us say you love a beautiful woman
whose obscurity you wish us to define.
Her name is Catharine, a petite child
who cannot sleep after sunrise.
She likes to hang her feet in rivers.
Tomorrow you will be married,
already the priest reaches
for vestments and homilies.
But tonight you hear in the wind
that Catharine is dead, raped, cut
from the cloth of your breathing
by the brother whose name is
in all your second-hand books.
After a while a pesky salesman comes
to whisper about his goods: honor,
revenge, lies and dull knives.
Until sunrise all you can think of
are unanswerable riddles, a game
to hide the mysterious ice in
Catharine's eyes. Later you hang
your feet in a river but it is
only wet and cold like the rain
sifting over you all night where
you have lain cool and quiet, barbed
on the hook at the end of a fine line.

The Sex of Poetry

She unzips her skirt, peels the nylons.
Her limbs are pale and smooth
as the back of a moving conch.
On this raw, conversational day
the crumpling articulation of her
underwear orchestrates her breath.
Beyond the window an impossibly
infinite vista spreads itself out.
The sea asserts all of its old reasons,
and contradicts, while you wait,
everything it tells you to trust.
Each single-minded water tuft
explodes its opposite as two terns
bank and tumble in an invisible wind.

At the corner of a field you remember,
your first girl lies down again,
those eyes staring up into the birch
that became a cage, her shy slender hands
easing back the plain cotton dress.
You stare at the lightening veins
of your wrist. Naked, tiny perturbations
of your cold skin will not go away
soon, disappear like any moment
that by the sea beats at your temples
like a madwoman's fists. You say that
now and know she doesn't care.

She doesn't want your life story
unless it leads to a new country.
Her tan is rich and warm. Cocked
against the window, her legs frame
sea light and her small-hair hangs
wild as grapevines. With her no one
will connect you to a good time.

If she has a name it is false.
As your tongue climbs her trunk,
what does it matter you can hear
fists of leaves beating down a street
swept by the sea? She rides you hard
and you forget to watch the boat
bobbing the horizon, dead in the water.
You love the shining sweat she wears.

Coming Attractions

Cynthia sits in the skimpy skin
of her brand-new nightgown,
her nakedness not subtle
as she recalls a dark angel
at the Queen City Drive-In,
which is where she has been,

and with him most of the night.
Had she wanted to watch movies
of Marlon Brando in fights?
Her angel kept hissing "Honey!"
She kept sliding between sight
of denouements and appetites

she didn't know she had. Tough
to keep her balance she whispers,
thinking of "Buster, that's enough"
though it wasn't by half.
She was saved by sudden trembles
of taillights and Brando's death.

Across the blazing lot plots
concluded in a rush, though
some calmly hung around.
Now Cynthia floats the town
in her gaze and exposes
something she should not,

some fresh thing discovered.
She sits like that for hours,
ignoring time and the motors
rooting the dark like lovers.
O angel, Cynthia's smeared
with joy and tiny flowers.

In the City of Wind

When I am drunk I may ask you to dance and give you
everything this life has given to me. Don't take it.
You will know who I am by the pine seed
in my nose, the mimosa fluting
all the way in the back where

there is also a '52 Chevy and the family I cannot find
in the photograph book which is all
I have left of my worldly goods.

Watch what I do with the casting forge: wheels, wheels,
pink ingots like babies spun from my hook, what they
taught me to do well before they kicked me out.
I know a man who said I could do it blind.
I believe that man said the God's truth.

Of all those I have fallen down with, I have died
for no one and do not want to die with Michigan
Avenue curbs to cuddle me. In my own life
I have cut down one who hung in a window

like a balding tire floating over the clay not far
from my lost Atlantic which has its own carcasses
to take care of. Chicago is a killer of drunks

who will kiss you for nothing, which is an angel's act.
I am no angel even blinded by the fury of wheels,
even sick for pines and cancerous women.
Just because I touch your coatsleeve
do you think I have nothing?

America, I worked my ass off for your piss-poor wine.
Sing to me now as you always claimed you would,
my life lies loose in my pocket like lint.

Dome Poem

Not, of course, the monster hunched downtown,
   with its rigid paws coiled into purchase
     where it seems to take a quiet shit,
    though it is certainly attractive enough,
with Parian marble and stained glass slits,

to tell us something if we looked close instead
   of up, dizzying ourselves until we forget
     what it was we were looking at it for or
    where we are. But no, not that Whitmanian
lump of what is bigger and better than other

such creations. What we must have is so simple
   it constantly sits there like a shadow's
     shadow on water, bones and tendons slyly
    hidden so only the maker knows how it is
done, and it smiles and says simplify, simplify.

It is so much like America, too, that anyone
   inside looks out uninhibited on the stars
     which suddenly become real and intense
    like the rain beating wherever we are
until it is a waterfall of original innocence,

even though there may be a syphilitic finger
   gouging a tender trench. What matters to
     us is the words it can nourish, hold,
    even generate like scribes in slow sweat,
row on row distilling the King James that no

one of them thought more worthy than his poems.
   But a poem is a kind of country, full
     of tent stays and lines you always kick
    at night, politicians and old women with
old eyes loving the transparent, cheap silk

anybody can use to set up one of those lean-to
  lily pads. The good thing about a dome
    is the way the principle reduces, extends
  one drop of water to its proto-shape, one
wounded round atom smashing back in vengeance

it has never conceived in its watery head.
  Splitting the atom reveals the absence
    neither heart nor mind can bear, air,
  whose stout shell the dome leans on, that
darkness in and out of rooms, mouths, words.

Pink Slip at Tool & Dye

He can only drink tea now, screwed and filed.
She is dead, in metal flecks.

55 years old and look like a bad nail
by God they yanked me out
I can tell you

soon as the hurt come son shut up
it don't mean nothing

but listen: you got time for a ride?

Habit's put the glass in his hands, the brown
tasteless tea, slime, and cigarettes.
Every Sunday the same, old dog
fat at his feet.

Ain't so much me I'm asking for
dog like to get out and piss
think they remember.

Near the main gate of Gary Steel I stop.
The amber light pours out of stacked horizons,
monstrous cranes hang over suburbs.

She think that piss mean something
it don't mean nothing.

Turning back in the dark, headlights flash
on our faces, bent, light of a woman's hair.

Figure from an Elder Lady

I

Don't women, Mr. Ransom, as much as geese
deserve a voice? Must we be tasked
with silence, be always the antecedents
of your pedantic? What is the purpose?

Think twice,

madam, then speak as befits
your station. I control myself in masks,
in loving birds, as Apollo did.
All surface consists of hide and grease.

Benign heart, your intelligence chafes
my passion and leaves it sharper.
It's possible you are wrong
to beget me with force
and nothing to say.
I want a divorce
from undainty birds that wander
through no time. My tongue
wants words hotter than you made.

Nothing sears

but fails; chills are the rule.

Yet early and late, must I be lost?
Why did you make plot with weather?
Why did you give old Conrad new tools
to heckle me in rhyme and meter,
to shake his fist at space?
I waited while,
disobedient, he jeered.

Fear.

II

Yes. Yours in Conrad's fist.
Grief as of a hung face
which the sweating soldier mistook
for nerves' tick, no worse,
so turned vaguely tired home.
Walking thus, suddenly afraid
of done and undone, he looked
for a shop to get drunk. Spades
already echoed on the road
where they rolled the rock.
Always whores, we were dismissed.

Back at the argument (I think
you might say, though not in lines)
           those Greek birds wink.
Conrad knew this. His belief in art's
exclusion I granted . . . is there time? . . .
to enforce the love I knew to be
our sequel, you. In what they are
these birds say the only story.
Conrad agrees, for I have asked him:
in verse a woman must depart
yet remain, essence of everything.

This is medieval stuff and indicts
my husband and my maker, but at last
I am the one who cries in goose and grief,
gardened with loss and no relief.
I give you words with artifice
that never could break ice.
You gave me this empty face,
Conrad's wife's. I wanted more.
Now I give it back as you go forth
from widow's arms, parsing crowns
of stars, unbent, puzzling device.

The Palmreader

I do not believe in Madame Margo's palm.
There is no earth smelling of rotted plums
between her thumb and the jeweled fingers.
This death she speaks of is a cheap one.
We all die. It is nothing to say that.
So that time when the others drank wine
on the way to her tent, I remained
alone by the bumping river, happy, light
from the fire telling me its true story
as the waterbugs skidded in chaos and fear.
Last night I dreamed of you once more.
I know what even Madame Margo does not know
and when I climb the hill for more wood
I find you are dancing away in little clouds
my breath makes. Do not be afraid of her,
do not think of this death she awards you.
I ask you, did you say look into the candle?
In the dream I saw you doing two things.
First you were sitting at a fire, then
you tried to find the waterbugs under rocks.
When you discover you are growing cold
you must immediately come to me. I will
tell you why your fingers are all naked.

One Question, Two Seasons

to Mary Alice Cornwell

I. Churchland Summer

That cemetery in the place hallowed by
its name, cramped like all cemeteries in the east,
overburied, overburdened ground, groaning with
deadly replicas of unlikely angels,

I have been back there in the stubbed wilting grass
burned brown as locusts on the oak's trunk,
but not often and never in winter
in the pulse of snow-whirl, and maybe
cold is not the season I have
to pack in and go for the feeling of what
comes to me all this blustery day, your hand
like the sea enormously cool in my fever. O that,

but not only that, the ur-anguish I have no word for.

Maybe in heat, with dust sinuous on the dirt roads,
dust grained and deep in the seat of my pants,
on my face like ashes.

I have cozened you from the roots of gardens,
found you in dim rooms down on your broad back.
I was out of breath, too, afraid to move.

There was plenty of dirt on that day, and heat,
yet I did lean late after midnight to whistle
an old song over the chair where the wool you
weaved knotted what warmth
a dying woman can keep in her breath,
and you were cold. I am as sure it was so
as the season you called black August.

Who is accused in this? Not that grass
parched, ticking where I came to stand in

the glib knock of the dirt where they pressed you
dry as a bulb while the cicadas wailed. Does anyone
with red eyes and stunned tongue understand this?

I don't care that you died, I want to keep alive
the love you made good in me. So who can tell me

how to stop dreaming those bones charred by cold,
the frame of the stripped skin,
the real absence of eyeholes?

II. Back River Winter

For some good time I mourned you only in walking
through heat-haze and the fat proud wild-flowers
where the fireflies waited for us to run.

But in winter which is infinitely young
with a rumpled white sheet that invites all
cessation to the tumbling pain in the nerves?

There are apples in the yard, red and soft.
Who would ask why they fell? What they say, buried
in their dark skins, their seeds more perfect than reason,

is less inaudible than weeping. I have some need
to speak of final things in my own tongue, perimeters
I must keep to like the cautious wheeling fishhawk

who eats the apples in bad times. Today in snow
I watched them peel a man from his tree-clenched car.
I saw the wrecker slide with its prize, go away

like a fat woman, like you, a kind of jolly dance
turned sour that with one finger I could blot out.
Then was gone. Was snow. Was mud bridging its wound

and not even a bluejay to break that vision. Yet
I did walk out by the river cheerfully feathering
the same sun I could pretend was my daughter's hair

and in pines knotting up odd shadows, believe it
or not, I could imagine I heard the promised Christ
beautifully breathing that dead man's name.

Tonight someone in the cold will ask as I ask
what is the trick of it? In this weather I think
I must learn how to walk out of despair, to see

what the apples fall into is a place without answer
or asking, and accept it as the fishhawk does, the man
who drives the wrecker and sings a song of one

woman he has not loved for the whole of a single night.
I must give over grief and begin in the winter
I love to love whatever believes in the good.

And if you should find me whistling your old fame
among great-grandchildren, remember it is what
you have taught me, and nothing less will I know.

The Gift of the Second Snow

When it stopped the sun suddenly poured through
the thorned black locusts and that boiling
slopped over those branches, quicksilvered
across the new lacy surf of the lawn,
rose up beyond the windowsill,
frothed against the glass
until I would let it in,
and though I huggered
at my abstract hurt
no thorns

I could feel snagged in any metaphysics
I spread out. I can tell you I was
unprepared for the swelling
your arms made at my neck
like a whispered joy.
Then I had to let out
the dog, turn off the TV,
give up my good excuse
to go on writing
hard things

and it was just then the children came
swaddled up like small pines, glittery,
speckled for their own celebrations,
their eyes pumping up
what was left of my heart,
so we went out for hotdogs,
and went all night on our
bellies under the black
locusts, until you
fell with me, soggy
in bed, in love,
in the dark.

The Spring Poem

Everyone should write a Spring poem.

Louise Gluck

Yes, but we must be sure of verities
such as proper heat and adequate form.
That's what poets are for, is my theory.
This then is a Spring poem. A car warms
its rusting hulk in a meadow; weeds slog
up its flanks in martial weather. April
or late March is our month. There is a fog
of spunky mildew and sweaty tufts spill
from the damp rump of a back seat. A spring
thrusts one gleaming tip out, a brilliant tooth
uncoiling from Winter's tension, a ring
of insects along, working out the Truth.
Each year this car, melting around that spring,
hears nails trench from boards and every squeak sing.

Picking Cherries

The ladder quakes and sways under me, old wood
I put too much faith in, like ancestors strained.
You circle me, cradling the baby, sun guttering
in your face, parading through the leaves, glad.
If I looked down I would see your calm fear, see
in your narrowed eyes my bones chipped, useless.
The bucket hangs from my belt, pulling obscenely
at my pants, but the cherries drop in and grow
one by one. I keep reaching higher than I need
because I want the one that tickles your tongue.
When I come down we will both be older, slower,
but what of that? Haven't we loved this climbing?
If the ladder gives way I still believe I can
catch one branch, drop the bucket and ease down.

Drunks

A poetry reading at the VA Hospital for the Rehabilitation of Addicts and Alcoholics, Battle Creek, Michigan

1.
Nobody on the lawns, the impeccable fairways.

That's what you drive through here.
Oh, maybe one man
pulls a golf cart. No clubs in his bag.
They do not allow clubs. He plays
in his head, smack, flight, and the gliding game.
Nobody with him,
nobody to say *Hey Buddy, watch your damn ball* or
Jesus, you blew it again.

Driving, you watch him shrink in your rearview
mirror. Alone. Keepers stay inside, warm, smart.
They watch. No clubs are allowed.

2.
Buildings hunch ahead ringed in shrub,
harsh evergreen. Snow domes that sad brick, windows
wear yellow even lids. Big doors grip like molars.
Grass ripples
so clean it seems unreal, dark as the swept shoulders
of businessmen who never tip the bootblacks because
they smell like bad wine or dirt.
Nobody moves.
No scraps, no letter fading, crumpled
at a curb, no cigarette wrapper hustles. You blow
stale breath on fingers suddenly cold, read numbers,

move on more afraid than you were. What do they want?
You say an uncle's name, one who was
fat, pink, and dead drunk.

59

3.

Past blighted elms, ragged pines, sharp winter sun
warms in their hands where they wait for you, anonymous
faces tight in that just-got-up cold splash.
                                        You drift around
curves, sink back toward the uncle, Biggie, his hand
     reaching for the bottle, the knife still
          whispering over your head, that flash as it

stabs the wall, missing you, missing the woman, but
     still hurting years after moss pressed its rag
          cold on Biggie's shattered veins. You track
               the limb-shadows and remember flat-bellied

college girls, good tans, skirts like mimosas, long ago.

4.

You don't expect the thin Negro who bolts across the lawn
shirtless. It's below freezing. You nose the car into space
marked *Reserved*. The man who comes out, a counselor,

says it is nobody, nobody. He leads you through wire cages,
past Coke and candy machines. The lights say empty, try
somewhere else. There, hands jammed in torn pockets, they
fall in behind you, their footsteps, yours, one sound.

If you asked who died someone would step out, step, then
turn away. One man crosses lawns like a shot gazelle,
his black woolly hair leaping.

5.

                    The counselor says you're the freak, rich writer.
                    He walks so keys jingle loudly on his belt.
                                        At the front of the room,
suddenly alone, you crack a window. Their eyes run over you
          cold open. They could stone you if one drunk
               screamed *Get him!* Nobody says a word.

You gulp cold coffee they bring, grin to the hands holding
    wooden ashtrays, tables that jerk
        uncontrollably.
                Biggie's nails always split
down the middle in the cold. Bad lumber, he whined, but
    he couldn't hit straight. The hammer's half-moons
    bloomed on his bones and his palms got used
    to coiling like claws.
                You open the book of poems.
6.
Wind seeps at your back but you sweat, watch white hair
like the crown-feathers of zoo birds, pheasants maybe,
rise and drift and fall. It would be easy to see a single man
break down and beg on a street corner, but not so many
as these. How many corners would it take?
                       They welcome you
because you come from the world with a corner for each one.
        Only the poem dies
and will not lie happily in the gutter. You make
    a curse like a cop's in their ears. Among
    soldiers you confuse the drab greens
    of this room with Day Rooms, Ward Rooms,
    jail-green drunk tanks. Wind seeps.
When they laugh you want to buy them all drinks.
    Instead you make bad jokes about hating
    Armies, about getting out one day.
                    Nobody laughs.
Nobody laughs.
        You push the window wider. No black gazelle,
only shrub grinding the brick. From here nobody can see
the golf course, the clubless player you admire
so casually. *They'll catch him downtown.* Why? *That's where*
    we go when we can. No place else to go. No money.
    No credit. They don't deliver here.

7.
Hey Bud them poems make you any money?
They drum their fingers, big high school rings, smoke, drink
coffee. They make you see they know what counts,
why you came here, writer, freak, but
make it easy, as if you were family
come home, made good, with poems full of money,
old street corners, cheap whiskey.

8.
You begin again. One in the back leans out
of an unstable dream, pokes his gray head behind a table
                              (Biggie's playing scary games
                              the neighbor's girl screamed.)
and tumbles, a whiskery heap. You whisper get up easy.
   He laughs first, the drunk's con, be funny,
      throw loud pies in your face for a drink; when laughs

   dribble off like spittle, his eyes dry grim,
      deep as corks slapped back in the bottleneck
         too many times. Your voice warps like a struck saw

through bar poems that say you want to take them home
   to the sweet greasy lights of taverns, cut
      back to smoke that holds the friend in pain,
         the war buddy, the dead guy that owes you.

         No money, no dice, no roll. You
      pour poems over the room like dollars
   burned, like the soft hips of women swaggering
with plates of beer in those flush, early hours.
                              Nobody laughs.

9.
Biggie couldn't read or write. He played Jew's harp.

One fat man in a polo shirt
three rows back puts his hand on his hip
and stands up mean as a beat walker, the hurt
on his forehead a thick red scar. He's quick
with hate. But words won't come first,
only fists. Then a torrent, curses
he's never said, shiny slugs. *Prick,*
he screams, *You're nobody. Who's worse
than you are? You come out here to get rich
on us. What do you care about drunks?* A girl
you hadn't seen appears beside him,
touches his arm, sits him down, whirls,
and disappears. You quiver, stick
cigarettes in your mouth. Hurt,
you wonder why you came. Sick,
you stumble through poems like closed doors.

10.
Three men break for coffee, cards in the room by the Cokes.
Later, when you leave, they laugh.

Bumming cash and cigarettes paid Biggie back. His shoe
split with a secret passage: *Boy that's for one
bottle for when I go.* Five bucks.

They'd never find it no matter how much they beat him.
They beat him dead,
dumped him on the porch. Neighbors passed that
night. Drunk, they said. Stupid, drunk.
We said he was drunk again.

They like your story.
Something between you now. Is that what they want?

11.
       Fictions. Drunk uncles left for dead.
    Scorn, loneliness, shame, pummeled brains, split
hands. What's left?
Butchered ambition, pawn tickets, old pictures
in wallets moldering like corpses. Hang on, hang on
to alleys, flush pimps, coldwater whores, both shoes.
They want anything to take back to the rooms where
you have to dream to stay alive: poems

               must smell like cash, stick like Coke to the skin,
               wear shedding coats, get the shakes, throw up
               on wives still loved, sing Country/Western

fictions. You read Hemingway's "Killers."
They know the world a battered boxer knows.
Ole Anderson makes them quake like hooked meat.
                         They understand killers
from the feet up. Ankle coats, suits full of holes.

You stop when the motorman enters the cafe: what now?

You make them writers, claim anybody
could come in that door, anybody, whatever they want.
They laugh, nobody fooled. Magically, they reach
for guns, turn ashtrays to sawed-off carbines.

Blow the mother's brains out!   Not anybody,

they know who's coming in. The fat one shouts: *Killers*
don't come for no reason. Anderson had it coming.

Bad break. Bad break.   Nobody says that.

12.
       Fictions. The room is dizzy with sheer breath. Alleys
   open now, somebody on the run, puking from the heart.

You go back to the poems.
                       On the sofa you fake sleep. Your aunt
                       follows Biggie out back, his rich shoe
                       dragging. *What do they want Biggie?*

13.
The next time you see Biggie dead drunk, dead.
Fictions. The counselor says
what you saw was nobody, nobody. That shadow runner
no shot gazelle, nobody.
                   You try to catch him
with poems for black angels, drunk angels, but too late.

They leave silent, in twos, threes: KP, toilets,
facts the boozeless need to live. Bad news.
One comes up alone, hands shy behind him. Does he know
who Ole Anderson ran from, or where Biggie went? You planned
to tell him thank you, but Anderson got away.
                       Would he believe it? No.
He's tall black. Green jungle fatigues, sunglasses
hide him like a secret in a rented room. He turns your hand
in the brother's grip, wants your name
on the torn flat of a buck pack.
                       Fictions.
You line it out in red.   Ask the angel's name,
he says, you'll find him sometime.

14.
     You drive out slowly, sweat-sodden, chilled so deep
you think no laughing drunk can ever make you warm again.
                    Odd black squirrels shoot down
      the elms, cross blind, gambling you'll stop and look.
      At the last corner there's a sign for traffic
      nobody remembers. Fairways are empty everywhere.

The counselor said few graduate for good. Graduate from
what you asked, but you were done and so was he.

15.
At every bar you pass you slow but see no sleek gazelle
face down like a man lining up a putt. Killers,
bristling silverfish rustle in your hair,
go nowhere but home to Biggie, singing on his porch,
his breath sweet vomit, his shoes rich and cold.

Somehow you know the corner where the angel is
and halfway home you stop and learn to say
the only name you ever knew, and find him
waiting alone, tears fat on the back of his hand,
crazy drunk, waving at the gaudy world like family.

Part III

Hole, Where Once in Passion We Swam

The sun frets, a fat wafer falling like a trap of failed mesh.
I watch the pin-glare of a mockingbird's eye cut sharply, descend
on the blank water, then emerge from himself naked
as a girl who shimmered here, once, for me.

If we come back like penitents to kneel over water, bass swirling,
scattering the mayflies that often, in silence, graze

lips, what is the word floating out from the mouth unbearable
as a bird's black grin or a madman's lust?

The word is not we, but *me*. Giving it again and again

brings no one out of the willows and I, willing to believe
like a sap in whatever dives or rises hear no voice
but the mist sizzling on stones. I lift my head

for echoes out of trees, for the flashed recoil of flesh hung
cheap and gaudy, wingless, above the stab of water
that crunched her like a beer can. Toads honk

the only answer. Among them, a boy, I felt

the grotesque pull of the moon all night, peeled and went slowly
down in terror, rising, falling through the pulpy leaves
until the sun caught me, drained, and I was no one
wanted, so walked away from all knowing,

walked into town and drank, calmly, an illegal beer, then slept.

The hooks, in hairy hands, clawed it smooth as a dish, a super-
human search by flood and fire light. What could they find?
Like many, I have been out of town a long time.

I wish the face floating above the chill at my knees opened
the door of a drab hotel. I wish it said *Go to hell*
or *Do you know what time it is*, anything

that, if I heard it, I could kneel to and swear to be faithful.

Sailing the Back River

Tonight no one takes fish. Tattered pennants
of T-shirts flap, their shadows riding wave crests,
among the hulls half-ashore and wholly sunken.
Always I am the waterman snagging nets on keels
in the graveyard of boats, the pale sailor who
glides with the music of nails through plank rot
and oil scum to sit in the toy wheelhouse of fathers.

I do not ask you to come with me or even to watch
the pennants signaling the drift of the winds.
Nothing I could do would raise one body bound
under these mud-struck beams, but I mean to do
what I can to save my own water-logged life and here
is the best place I know to beg. I throw out love
like an anchor and wait where the long houselights
of strangers tickle the river's back. I go alone

as a creaky-boned woman goes to the far bench
at the heart of her garden where the rose suffers.
There will be time for you to hold in your palm
what each has held here, the sudden canting of gulls,
a room with one back-broken chair, the pot-belly
sputtering as it answers the wind, the soft knock
waters make at the fair skin of roots. I come here
to stop up my lying words: your life was always bad.

Isn't it right to drag the rivers for the bodies
not even the nets could catch? I won't lie, I want
you to lie with me on the tumbling surface of love.
This is the place to honor crab song, reed's aria,
where every hour the mussel sighs *begin again*. Say
I am water and learn what I hold as river, creek,
lake, ditch or sewer. I am equal with fire and ice.
We are one body sailing or nothing. My life, yours,
what are they but hulls homing, moving the sand?

Back River Easter

The babies from Cumberland are dying, mister.
You know the question that everybody asks
over the oysters, the crabs, the whiskey:

after all these years, and you making good cash,
why for Christ's sake have you turned up now?
What kind of answer can you hang on that?

I think of blue hydrangeas, a woman's form,
the river they are all going to die by soon
if they survive small defeats in the shipyard.

Where are the answers to all the questions
not asked? I come back mumbling at death,
cursing church, lilies, and no resurrection

strong as the spring tides that know how to lift
when they want any lover's good-looking girl
who was buried by pines in her fever and fits.

I should have been one kneeling in boots and boats
but she made me leave the stink of baitshacks,
the teeth of clamrakes harping the old bones.

The babies from Cumberland got winded, people.
I drink in her house that once was so upright
and repent one crazy Christmas when the three

cons and I stole cheap wine then kissed her
into sleep. She said she dreamed the Mallard
none of us could knock down with that .22 pistol.

How answer now her old lies, her waddling gait
when they hurt me? I swear I'm not loving you
bastards anymore, even if you die in her wake.

I say that for her to an assembly of worms
and the sexton slips in with a shovel to split
the marsh for Cumberland's baby come to term.

The Perspective and Limits of Snapshots

Aubrey Bodine's crosswater shot of Menchville,
Virginia: a little dream composing a little water,
specifically, the Deep Creek flank of the Warwick.
Two-man oyster scows lie shoulder to shoulder,
as if you walk them, one land to another,
no narrow channel hidden in the glossy middle
like a blurred stroke, current grinning at hulls.
It is an entirely eloquent peace, with lolling
ropes and liquid glitter, this vision of traffic
and no oystermen in sight. Clearly, Bodine is not
Matthew Brady catching the trenchant gropes frozen
at Fredericksburg with a small black box. So well
has he excluded the neat Mennonite church, yachts,
country club pool, the spare smell of dignity seeps.
Perhaps it is because of the zoom on the teeth
of the oyster tongs; perhaps it is after all Sunday.

Above the last boat, the flat-faced store squats
at the end of the dirt road as if musing over
accounts receivable. No doubt it has weathered
years of blood spilling. A spotted hound lifts
his nose above what must be yesterday's trash fish,
his white coat luminous against deep foliage. What
Bodine fails to see is the dog turning to lope
uphill under that screen of poplars, behind fat
azaleas that hide the county farm and the drunks
pressed against wire screens, sniffing the James.
One oysterman thumped his noisy wife (the window
was accidental) because she had a knife and mourned
their boy twenty years drowned. If he knew Bodine
stood at the marsh tip where his boy dove, if he
were but told a camera yawned to suck in the years
of his worst sailing shame, he would turn away. He

would whistle up boys in the dust that is dignity
and if he could he would spit in his hand and tell
his nameless black cellmate there are many men
for whom the world is neither oyster nor pearl.

Where We Are Today, You Will Notice Is

Flecks of dust black as pepper in the tricky sun
that, at the ridge, deflects from pines

leaves the little creek you go down to dull,
gray as its grated bottom. No green
word describes what floats
there, a kind of spinach,

tatters of the heart, infinitely soft because
this is one of those places the light
moves through like a monk,
obsequious, everything

the numinous reminder of how what lives leans
with currents, out of the dark, wants
to burst the cowl of habit

become blossom, but could not, would dry out
exposed, and drift, stiffened,
like music badly remembered.

Patria mea est rises as you kneel for a close look;
faces, a girl and a woman, skid like waterbugs,
flakes you cannot hold

like the blown flags under water. One
word, missing, nags you up the cold stone

where light cracks like the cooling tractor.
It follows you into the kitchen, across linoleum
worn like marble, hangs

with the dying vine in the window. You cradle
the coffee and the bread, then predict rain.
The woman, brittle as the earth,

gives you her back, biting it off. "Good."

Some Good Luck in Lightfoot

There is something else. Once I woke up in the bed
of a farmer's hog-dungy truck because in a bar
I said I hoped I would die in the lick of the James
and he said "I taken you home for the reason
who'd know but you was dumb enough to do just that?"

Most people don't believe there are men keeping sisters
prowling their attics. He was one.
What I know about wanting not to go nuts, about how
to love my own simple life, I take from two
whose speech came like windows scraping.

Mostly she was locked up good and he would talk
as we wandered up the tiny stairs and walked
through the gallery of girls she sketched
on sheets and tacked to the eaves. He shook
his head for the purity of what she made, although
she dreamed plain: each girl wore green as she did,

the rent streak of the crayon blurring into the hubs
of spinning wheels always there, and legs skewed out
like bad-cut boards and faces facing to a window
hardly more than a butter smear. Two weeks
I heard him whisper through the hole in his throat

the neighbors must not know or else they'd think
being crazy's just the joke the artist plays.
As serious as if he'd laid a knife on a hog's throat
he swore that art was the only thing that mattered
in this moony world. *You saw it? Didn't you see it!*
Upstairs she thumped her boards and drooled.

Maybe like him I would want to die for art's cash.
He said that, too. He was wrong.
What good is the passion that keeps a woman
croaking for a man with more than one screw loose
and lines her life with infinite angles of pain?

When I left he warned me to keep away from the James
and I have done the best I can in a hundred towns
where no one took me home to keep me living. You
would be wrong to think I do not love
the way that woman soared in shades of green.

Si Hugget, Drifting, Ruptured

Maybe some destroyer way out sent the wave,
the sea will carry such news without a man's asking,
maybe the net was too heavy and I slipped.
It could have been that, by God.

I don't know what it was. I was alive
and the sun hung on my face like a bruise one day
in 1945 when no Japanese gave up on a black island
that wasn't my own Egg Island Bar but
could have been the way it knocked me out.

What it is is a hole you can't even see. I do not want
to talk about this rupture or why the wife
of my two boys who was once thin as a bowline
has begun to stink like a rotting hawser.
We are like Diggs's funeral advertisement,
Ever Faithful To One High Standard.

Both boys came home in a box. You could put your fist
in the holes they wore and she has been a little
nervous ever since. Why shouldn't she
hold something back? What's
the meaning of waste, anyway?

I'll tell you what I know. The smell of salt is good
but the sea is nobody's friend. I don't know
what my boys smell like now but I see
the two of them stuffing their shirts
way up in the wedge of the bow,
after clams and I don't know what all.

I don't have the words to say this out plain, forgive me.

I was alive and then I was hurt and then I was dead
and then I was alive, that's how it was.
I see her drying the boys but I don't

see the wave coming which was when
the last thing I heard was a gull.

If you woke up staring into a scaled, stinking pile
of shirts not worth a good damn, the sun
boiling out of your life, hurt so bad
you don't know how to get home,
wouldn't you wonder why?

I cut my nets loose, I drifted, I said to no one
Jesus, what rotten thing have I done now?

Crabbing on the Hand Line

Somewhere behind me the clank and jerk of a crane clears
  houses,
echoing like weightlifters in bare rooms. Water fills
basements where families once muscled like schools
of fish. The yachts bob in neat lines, gleaming

in the big plate glass window of the new country club. Gulls peck
a meal from the disgorged mud. I hear the squeege of black
tires taking the buffets of water,

protecting the white, pure flanks. Later, there is the cross
of a sailboat's mast and, underwater, the moons
of portholes bulged eerily

like crab eyes. Crabs can't see. They live by smelling
the rotten hunk of a chicken's neck. I toss it out like a bribe,
careful to make no sudden noise, cast no shadow.

They have arms like Samson and I, only ten, know that pull
from the water has to go through fingertips transmitting
the stretch and tear of flesh without sound or shape
and will be what it means to stand staring
in the sun, hungering for yachts.

It means waiting while cranes smash your house. Waiting.

Where I have come from, why, does not reveal itself anymore
until the sun burns me back to three black children,
older and larger, who will beat my ass again

in this memory, who will bebop something I don't know how to
  say.
Listen, the mud clots my eyes. Bleeding, I watch them
scramble uphill through gulls, the slide
I know only in scream already started.

When I go home someone will ask what has turned me black all
  over.

79

I cannot give them crabs or answer anything for years.
They will whip me again.

All night I dream of big arms jerking chunks of white meat, black
dreams filling my room with wheeze and bang, my hand paying
out the crab line that breaks for the last time.

Two black children are crying like gulls, mud-skinned like me,
for one whose eyes bump blindly at the moons of the white
hull where the long-armed mast sways. I wish I could
tell them my father will come and save the one.

who for a joke stole all I ever caught before the mud
gave way and the sun, shining on his hand,
sank,

but I am only ten,
too small to climb the crane where my father grins.

Eastern Shore: Smith Island

Am I at home here, humpback nub,
          nub of nothing, rock where pines
preen in wimpling winds,
          roots with capillaries bulged,
sucking seamist to live? I oar out
          anyway, wallow through troughs,
go where brothers, fathers lie
          and won't speak, dreaming, too, and
landing, lug the rowboat oafishly
          onto an island I can circle three
times each hour, barely running,
          reeds, mucksuck oozing my feet,
the only one today to love these
          lovely hulls. Yet how at home
where nobody lives? Who is the one
          whose body I row through the sun?
When I set out I meant to fish
          on the clean beach, cast with killdeer
going insane in that pas de deux
          the black waves banter, under-
cutting the stage they tick on. But
          I have no rod, am no fisherman in this
bronze October light. Scrambling from
          deck to deck, on the shells of dead
fishermen's boats, I feel the families
          pulling back alive while tides bubble
through stoved-in sterns. Silence
          in this junkyard of currents rots,
reeks, absorbs bleached carcasses of
          trout, jellyfish, lung-busted oysters,
sea-going Bugeyes with impeccable
          equality. The elements are everywhere
rising, meager flecks of flesh decomposing
          on spears of wood, glittery chips

wedged like gold in the ventricles of weed.
                    I run. I came here not to be alone,
to belly-flop, tripped forward on my face,
                    running blindly, as if to catch
some image of myself, some clown I greet
                    in a shard of windshield, whose big
feet I keep running into. Today, balance
                    snatched by a fool's tide in my head,
I caught my toes, stuck, hooked in the rot-
                    blossoming head a confused grandfatherly
turtle eased out in the wrong place
                    at the wrong time. Cartwheeling, flying
backward into his blood-rush, my mouth gives
                    its kiss to a reed-beard. I tumble
into holes where deep-set irises blinked
                    against huge buffetings of cold steel
flukes that might have been a killer
                    whale's. I breathe that stale, distant
death not quite relinquished from an island
                    floater hollowed by the brass wheel
of home-bound oyster scows. That's what
                    it means to come up dumbly wrong, fixed
in the deceptive cock-sure self's notion
                    of navigation. A being empties all over
again heart, fish-stuffed gut, still
                    threshing bones, its jaw snapping nothing
where I lay full-length as Gulliver. Sun
                    bleeds through the rear slope of his
house, warming sand crabs who come waving
                    one weak claw, gropers digging their
wind-beaten, juice-stewing bodies, tiny
                    silhouettes making cave shadows against
what weirdly transforms from heroic swimmer
                    to storm-proof charnel house for crabs.

And who lives here? Who gets up in that
            simple click of survivors, skin sored
with fresh blood, and holding a nose, goes
            to the lock-rattling boat at the island's
edge?
        Most days I leave with no answer
            I did not always have, let tide pull take
the channel to the pulsed light in a widow's
            window, and row until the salt crescents
my cheeks. By night silver squibs, Spanish
            Mackerels, dance in the air as if dredged
from dreams. Unseen, they plummet dead-
            pan like old jokes on darkened stoops.
Tonight, halfway across, my arms sag, oars
            drift and tell of thunderstruck turtles
turned senseless in their wakes. It is
            the dead calm of tide turn that possesses
me to leap up, straddle the seat planks,
            rock until I thump out a swell of paddle
percussion for the half-headless, wholly
            homeless floaters stunned on course, and
becoming what they never thought of—
            what the ghostly radar of crabs homes at,
claims, turns to a new temple, enters,
            claws high, no grief, no joy imagined.
In darkness, I slap a tune for dark ones
            who eat and breed and age in hoods
they surrender to the meat of the living.

Looking for the Melungeon

Rounding a slip of the marsh, the boat skids
under me and the propeller whines naked,
then digs and shoots me forward. A clapper rail
disappears in reeds and one crane, shaken
from his nap blinks, and holds.

He makes me think of the Lost Tribe of Virginia,
as if the scree of insects were the Jew's
harp in John Jacob Niles's mouth.

A creek opens its throat and I enter, dragging
down to hear my wake's slip-slop,
thinking of the man who warned me people
were the same everywhere, lost and wondering

how they came to the life no one else wanted.
Sweet Jesus, he was right. Now he lies
in this sodden ground for the first time
in his life and I do not know even where.

Today is no different, the waters flood hulks
of empty houses, leaving beer cans to gleam
in the indifferent moon. The first stalks of
narcissus break the ground with gold
though March still means tonight to freeze.

I know this place, its small mustering of facts
wind-worn and useless, real and repeated, the same
anywhere. At the end the creek leads to a room,
one placid boat swinging at a stick, pines sieving

air, the cleat ringing like small jewelry.

The Cunner in the Calotype

You need to know these boats, cunners, square
of bow and stern, never painted, always with a bottle
floating where the bilge is always rank and deep.
Sometimes they hold the sun like a butter tub but
nobody ever stepped a sail in one. They're used
to ferry out to where the oyster scows squat, sere
and long as a lovely woman's thigh in an old dream.
You need to ask why they lie cracked, sucking salt
water through the reed tubes, what has happened
to shove them back into the center of the marsh
where the scree of gnats goes out when a fisherman,
desperate in the end, shoves his finger in his ear.
You need to hear the slow toll of rope ends, mossed
like drifting arms, the bell-cry of cleat and chained
transom stained a hundred hues by the licking sea.

When the dozers come to take the marsh, slapping down
layers of asphalt, when the all-temperature malls and
the good women of the garden club cease designing,
they will be gone, claimed by antique freaks, smashed
for scrap, the creeks leveled, the sun deceived with
only steel to flash on in the heat. They're unemployed,
no swimming boys will sink them for a joke, no wind
whip and toss them in a storm or leave them in a tree.
The fishermen exchange their good hard poverty for jobs
behind counters; few men ever rowed a boat on dirt and
what you'd get for one is not enough for one week's beer.
It is for this, because you need to know, I give you
the last cunner of all, its charred bottom still whole,
crabs and other creatures not yet gone, a man's hat
floating in the black water as if mislaid, going down.

What the Waterman Prayed

for John Haislip

I never asked for money, that's one thing.
I asked to see some good, a simpleton's act
of sense in all his sins. I never asked not
to die, only for grace to do it right. Who
asks for the woman that makes a man whole?
She gave me eight children in the same bed,
two girls who sank the boats I carved in love.
When both married bad I never asked for help
they couldn't give themselves. We live
in rooms whose shades are cracked by time.
I, being of sound mind, hope none of us die
until tomorrow or next week. Hope is not
prayer, which is all the truth I know.
I've been down on my knees, up to my ass
in knees, but my two girls died. I did not.
It wasn't prayer that helped me fail
the lives I've held. The roar in my head
tolls wind over water, a way of talking
to that rolling dark where I learned
what judgment is. It means casting nets
in depths great enough to lose your fear
when something's deeper yet to lose. Sons
will always pray not to hear I'm drunk again,
Job come home with his bewildered heart.
Men learn the things they can't pray out of.

I will not pray with any preacher in a robe.
Bad wind is what their wine won't wash away.
Who has his peace struck in a sudden light
lies stunned with luck and shattered love.
In a hundred fogs I've held my hands before
my face to catch ways the weather went,
always thinking there was time to change,
to be in wind the gull's tuning arc.

I've sailed my daddy's daddy's boat, worked
the same holes that fed them into men, who
both sank hard in simple beds and cursed
the life they left. No preacher makes
a man safe to see, in water, what he is.
I've prayed, for Christ's sake, breaking
wind in March storms that never raked
the leeches from my bitter heart, prayed
for nets not bagged with slime, but fish.
I know who found the man I thought I was
and he is sick for slants of sun playing
on a floor where children float like corks.
He prays to the stink of what's left to rot
when the tide is out on the black mud, to
wake himself for one more damned chance of
life. But that's not prayer. Maybe it is
not even hope, which never changed the wind
or put a lucky dollar in an old man's pocket,
or fished it out for a girl's gift in church
in the time before time howled headlong.

Looming: An Address to Matthew Fontaine Maury

In Cumberland I had one uncle
who couldn't get out fast enough, so split
his head on the gearcase of a LaSalle.

He did not die but said he remembered the dark
was like it must be when you are keelhauled.

Beyond him, in your time, there was a man
with my own blood who leaped from a mountain
because the tiny river was too green to bear.

These are stories of outsiders choked up
with delusions and the downhill nights of mines.
I hope they have found a country to live in

as I stand sighing over the cat's fur of the sea,
thinking of you gone from Virginia, skidding
like a skimmed stone in the half-light of exile.

Because no one recalls how the murmur of water
called you from the hills, because the light
of farmhouse and sea towns blew out
at your coming, because you loved

the humped backs of dolphin and whale
more than mother or father, because in high gales
you knew what it was to go drunk in the ropes,

because the Labrador and the Gulf Stream whisper
their secrets to you like a friend, I stand
here naming each blade of grass

for one America drove into the sea,
that claw-sucking beast indifferent as haze,
licking the yellow onion of the moon!

When the Fiddlers Gather

Now they are become more than men we must know how
to tune up, to take
their flying root-and-stem light of joy
from each old hand as it pumps under the dunesigh
and liver-spotted leaf, learn
from lean gray men
hunched on a rail and singing to the waters the beauty
of breezeless gull-dotted dusk.

This one, his time come, nods, clamped jawbones
patient as a crab's,
years of notes loosed now, ear tufts and
silver hair drifting like streamweed, sways, pours
down his last gamboling sweat
for the world to out-
sing itself. Then another from the bed of his leg
lifts fiddle, begins to cuddle

and counterstroke the dying-out strain that a gone
grandfather sang to
the end like a man fearing God (so cries
the tune-whipped and untucked brother of their
right hand). When he buckles,
the next bows quickly
in feeling his boots already tapping the dark line
of the hewn fence. It must be

like entering a world where every breath turns dead
reckless and pure as gull
song tuned by nothing but ribbed sealight,
where hard-headed laid-down fathers rise up slowly
among crocus and bluebell as if
only minutes before
sleep whined like a gnat. And it could be standing
simply in the lightning-

like motions of such nameless, hardly to be believed
angels, we come at last
into the unfretting wish to be nothing else,
for there rises from bow's graze and struck strings
not only land's lute, but eerie rapture
stunning the sailor
who feels at first daybreak a peace slicing wrist-labor
as if before storm or prayer.

Night Fishing for Blues

Fortress Monroe, Virginia

The big-jawed Bluefish, ravenous, sleek muscle slamming
into banked histories of rock
    pile, hair-shaggy pier legs, drives
    each year to black Bay shallows, churns,

       fin-wheels, convoys, a black army, blue

stained sequins rank after rank, fluting bloodshot
gill-flowers, sucking bitter land water, great Ocean
Blues with belly-bones ringing like gongs.

       Tonight, not far from where Jefferson Davis

hunched in a harrowing cell, gray eyes quick
as crabs' nubs, I come back over planks
deep drummed under boots, tufts of hair

floating at my ears, everything finally right
    to pitch through tideturn and mudslur
    for fish with teeth like snapped sabers.

       In blue crescents of base lights, I cast hooks

baited with Smithfield ham: they reel, zing,
plummet, coil in corrosive swirls, bump on
scum-skinned rocks. No skin divers prowl here,

       visibility an arm's length, my visions

hand-to-hand in the line's warp. A meat-
baited lure limps through limbs nippling the muck,
silhouettes, shoots forward, catches a cruising Blue

       sentry's eye, snags and sets

case-hardened barbs. Suddenly, I am not alone:
    three Negroes plump down in lawn chairs, shudder-
    casting into the black pod plodding under us. One

ripples with age, a grandmotherly obelisk,

her breath puffing like a coal stove. She swivels
heavily, chewing her dark nut, spits thick juice
like a careful chum.
When I yank the first Blue
she mumbles, her eyes roll far out on the black-
blue billowing sea-screen. I hear her canting

to Africa, a cluck in her throat, a chain

song from the fisherman's house. I cannot
understand. Bluefish are pouring at me in squads.
I haul two, three at a time, torpedoes, moon-shiners,
jamming my feet into the splintered floor, battling
whatever comes. I know I have waited
a whole life for this minute. Like purple dreams

graven on cold cell walls, Blues walk over

our heads, ground on back-wings, grind their teeth.
They splash rings of blue and silver around us, tiaras
of lost battalions. I can smell the salt of ocean
runners as she hollers *I ain't doing so bad
for an old queen.* No time to answer. Two

car-hoods down her descendants swing sinewy arms

in Superfly shirts, exotic butterflies: I hear them
pop beer cans, the whoosh released like stale breath
through a noose no one remembers. We hang

fast flat casts, artless, no teasing fishermen,

beyond the book-bred lures of the pristine streams,
speeded-up, centrifugal, movie machines rewound
too far, belts slipped, gears gone, momentum

hauling us back, slinging lines, winging wildly

as howitzers. Incredibly it happens: I feel
the hook hammer and shake and throw my entire weight
to dragging, as if I have caught the goddamndest

Blue in the Atlantic. She screams: *Oh my God!*

Four of us fumbling in beamed headlight and blue
arclight cut the hook from her face. Gnats butterfly,
nag us: I put it in deep and it must be gouged out
like a cyst. When it is free, I hear Blues not yet

dead flopping softly. I tell her it is a lucky
thing she can see. She mops blood blued over
gold-lined teeth and opens her arms so her dress

billows like a caftan. She wants

nothing but to fish. I hand her her pole, then cast
as far as I can. She pumps, wings a sinker and hooks
into flashing slop and reels hard. In one instant both

our lines leap rigid as daguerreotypes; we have

caught each other but we go on for the blue blood of
ghosts that thrash in the brain's empty room.
We pull at shadows until we see there is nothing, then
sit on the shaky pier like prisoners. Coil after coil
we trace the path of Bluefish-knots backward,

unlooping, feeling for holes, giving, testing,

slapping the gnats from our skins. Harried, unbound,
we leap to be fishers. But now a gray glow
shreds with the cloud curtain, an old belly-fire

guts the night. Already the tide humps around

on itself. Lights flicker like campfires in duty windows
at Ft. Monroe. She hooks up, saying *Sons they done
let us go.* I cast once more but nothing bites. Everywhere

a circle of Blues bleaches, stiffens

in flecks of blood. We kneel, stuff styrofoam
boxes with blankets of ice, break their backs
to keep them cold and sweet, the woman gravely
showing us what to do. By dawn the stink has passed

out of our noses. We drink beer like family.

All the way home thousands of Blues fall from my head,
falling with the gray Atlantic, and a pale veiny light
fills the road with sea-shadows that drift in figure

eights, knot and snarl and draw me forward.

POETRY FROM ILLINOIS

History Is Your Own Heartbeat
Michael S. Harper (1971)

The Foreclosure
Richard Emil Braun (1972)

The Scrawny Sonnets and Other Narratives
Robert Bagg (1973)

The Creation Frame
Phyllis Thompson (1973)

To All Appearances: Poems New and Selected
Josephine Miles (1974)

Nightmare Begins Responsibility
Michael S. Harper (1975)

The Black Hawk Songs
Michael Borich (1975)

The Wichita Poems
Michael Van Walleghen (1975)

Tracking
Virginia R. Terris (1976)

Cumberland Station
Dave Smith (1976)